Andrew Brodie Basics

LET'S DO MULTIPLICATION AND DIVISION

FOR AGES 10-11

with over **100** reward stickers

- Over 400 practice questions
- Regular progress tests
- Matched to the National Curriculum

Published 2016 by Bloomsbury Publishing Plc
50 Bedford Square, London, WC1B 3DP

www.bloomsbury.com

Bloomsbury is a registered trademark of Bloomsbury Publishing Plc

ISBN 978-14729-2638-8

Copyright © 2016 Bloomsbury Publishing
Text copyright © 2016 Andrew Brodie
Cover and inside illustrations of Maurice the Mouse and Andrew Brodie
© 2016 Nikalas Catlow. Other inside illustrations © 2016 Cathy Hughes

A CIP catalogue for this book is available from the British Library.

10 9 8 7 6 5 4 3 2 1

Printed in China by Leo Paper Products

This book is produced using paper that is made from wood grown in managed, sustainable forests. It is natural, renewable and recyclable. The logging and manufacturing processes conform to the environmental regulations of the country of origin.

To see our full range of titles visit **www.bloomsbury.com**

BLOOMSBURY

Introduction

This is the sixth in the series of *Andrew Brodie Basics: Let's Do Multiplication and Division* books. Each book contains more than 400 maths questions, deliberately designed to cover the following key aspects of the 'Number' section of the National Curriculum:

- Number and place value
- Multiplication and division.

Your child will get the most out of this series if you make time to discuss number knowledge as well as basic multiplication and division questions with them. Talk about real life situations, such as how many eggs there would be in sixteen boxes of six. Does your child recognise that the question can be split into a) finding the number of eggs in ten boxes and b) finding the number in six boxes, then adding together the two answers? Mathematically, this can be shown as $16 \times 6 = 10 \times 6 + 6 \times 6$. This is known as the Distributive Law.

You should also encourage your child to consider remainders in a real-life context: for example, if a box contains six eggs, how many egg boxes would be needed for thirty-one eggs? You could fill five boxes, but there would be a remainder of one egg. Give other examples, such as: I need to share thirty-one bars of chocolate between six children, how many bars do they have each? Here, each child can have five whole bars, but the final bar could be split into six equal pieces: now each child can have $5\frac{1}{6}$ bars of chocolate – the remainder has been used.

In Year 6 it is important that children continue to practise the times tables together with the related division facts: they should be able to fluently recite all of the times tables, from two to twelve, up to twelve times twelve. They will use their tables knowledge to identify multiples, factors and prime numbers, as well as square numbers and cube numbers.

The level of difficulty is increased gradually throughout the book but note that some questions are repeated, particularly in Brodie's Fast Fives. This is to ensure that children have the opportunity to learn vital new facts: they may not know the answer to a particular question the first time they encounter it, but this provides the opportunity for you to help them learn it for the next time that they come across it. Don't be surprised if they need to practise certain questions many times.

You may find that your child is challenged by some questions. Make sure that they don't lose confidence. Instead, encourage them to learn from their mistakes.

In Year 6, children use the facts they already know to solve related questions. They solve problems involving multiplication and division, and they practise multiplying numbers up to four digits by a one-digit or two-digit number, using the processes of short multiplication and long multiplication. They practise short division, dividing numbers up to four digits by a one-digit number, finding remainders where appropriate, and they extend their skills by learning the process of long division.

Children gain confidence by learning facts that they can use in their work. With lots of practice they will see their score improve and will learn to find maths both satisfying and enjoyable.

Look out for...

Maurice the Mouse, who provides useful tips and helpful advice throughout.

Brodie's Fast Five, quick-fire questions designed to test your child's mental arithmetic.

Do you know your times tables?

1 **Write out the tables facts as fast as you can. Time yourself.**

1 x 2 =	1 x 3 =	1 x 4 =	1 x 5 =
2 x 2 =	2 x 3 =	2 x 4 =	2 x 5 =
3 x 2 =	3 x 3 =	3 x 4 =	3 x 5 =
4 x 2 =	4 x 3 =	4 x 4 =	4 x 5 =
5 x 2 =	5 x 3 =	5 x 4 =	5 x 5 =
6 x 2 =	6 x 3 =	6 x 4 =	6 x 5 =
7 x 2 =	7 x 3 =	7 x 4 =	7 x 5 =
8 x 2 =	8 x 3 =	8 x 4 =	8 x 5 =
9 x 2 =	9 x 3 =	9 x 4 =	9 x 5 =
10 x 2 =	10 x 3 =	10 x 4 =	10 x 5 =
11 x 2 =	11 x 3 =	11 x 4 =	11 x 5 =
12 x 2 =	12 x 3 =	12 x 4 =	12 x 5 =

Time taken Seconds

Time taken Seconds

Time taken Seconds

Time taken Seconds

Here are the multiples of 2 up to 100.

2 4 6 8 10 12 14 16 18 20 22 24 26 28 30 32 34 36 38 40 42 44 46 48 50 52
54 56 58 60 62 64 66 68 70 72 74 76 78 80 82 84 86 88 90 92 94 96 98 100

Here are the multiples of 3 up to 100.

3 6 9 12 15 18 21 24 27 30 33 36 39 42 45 48 51 54 57 60 63 66 69 72 75 78
81 84 87 90 93 96 99

2 **Write the multiples of 4 up to 100.**

3 **Write the multiples of 5 up to 100.**

3

Do you know the three times table?

1 Write out the tables facts as fast as you can. Time yourself.

1 x 6 =	1 x 7 =	1 x 8 =	1 x 9 =
2 x 6 =	2 x 7 =	2 x 8 =	2 x 9 =
3 x 6 =	3 x 7 =	3 x 8 =	3 x 9 =
4 x 6 =	4 x 7 =	4 x 8 =	4 x 9 =
5 x 6 =	5 x 7 =	5 x 8 =	5 x 9 =
6 x 6 =	6 x 7 =	6 x 8 =	6 x 9 =
7 x 6 =	7 x 7 =	7 x 8 =	7 x 9 =
8 x 6 =	8 x 7 =	8 x 8 =	8 x 9 =
9 x 6 =	9 x 7 =	9 x 8 =	9 x 9 =
10 x 6 =	10 x 7 =	10 x 8 =	10 x 9 =
11 x 6 =	11 x 7 =	11 x 8 =	11 x 9 =
12 x 6 =	12 x 7 =	12 x 8 =	12 x 9 =

Here are the multiples of 6 up to 100.

6 12 18 24 30 36 42 48 54 60 66 72 78 84 90 96

2 Write the multiples of 7 up to 100.

3 Write the multiples of 8 up to 100.

4 Write the multiples of 9 up to 100.

The 25 times table is really easy and really useful!

1 Write out the tables facts as fast as you can. Time yourself.

1 x 10 =	1 x 11 =	1 x 12 =	1 x 25 =
2 x 10 =	2 x 11 =	2 x 12 =	2 x 25 =
3 x 10 =	3 x 11 =	3 x 12 =	3 x 25 =
4 x 10 =	4 x 11 =	4 x 12 =	4 x 25 =
5 x 10 =	5 x 11 =	5 x 12 =	5 x 25 =
6 x 10 =	6 x 11 =	6 x 12 =	6 x 25 =
7 x 10 =	7 x 11 =	7 x 12 =	7 x 25 =
8 x 10 =	8 x 11 =	8 x 12 =	8 x 25 =
9 x 10 =	9 x 11 =	9 x 12 =	9 x 25 =
10 x 10 =	10 x 11 =	10 x 12 =	10 x 25 =
11 x 10 =	11 x 11 =	11 x 12 =	11 x 25 =
12 x 10 =	12 x 11 =	12 x 12 =	12 x 25 =

Here are the multiples of 10 up to 200.

10 20 30 40 50 60 70 80 90 100 110 120 130 140 150 160 170 180 190 200

2 Write the multiples of 11 up to 200.

3 Write the multiples of 12 up to 200.

4 Write the multiples of 25 up to 500.

5

Time yourself completing the square.

Fill in the missing answers. Some have been done for you.

x	7	3	6	4	9	12	8	11	2	5	10	25
8				32								
11											110	
3												
10												
5												125
9						108						
2												
7												
12												
6					54							
25												
4												

Time taken

Seconds

Brodie's Fast Five

500 ÷ 10 =   400 ÷ 25 =

100 ÷ 20 =   150 ÷ 25 =   300 ÷ 20 =

Sometimes divisions have remainders.

There are 34 eggs. The eggs need to be sorted into boxes with 6 in each.

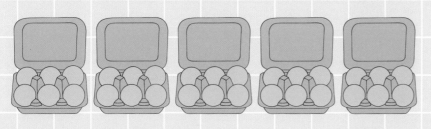

There are enough eggs for five boxes of 6, and there are 4 eggs left over.

We can write the mathematical sentence like this: $34 \div 6 = 5$ r4

This letter r means remainder.
The remainder shows what is left over.

Now try these.

1	63 ÷ 5	=
2	26 ÷ 3	=
3	51 ÷ 4	=
4	83 ÷ 6	=
5	53 ÷ 7	=
6	68 ÷ 5	=
7	100 ÷ 8	=
8	89 ÷ 9	=
9	101 ÷ 25	=

10	101 ÷ 12	=
11	101 ÷ 11	=
12	101 ÷ 2	=
13	101 ÷ 8	=
14	101 ÷ 4	=
15	101 ÷ 6	=
16	101 ÷ 5	=
17	101 ÷ 30	=
18	101 ÷ 40	=

Brodie's Fast Five

240 ÷ 12 =   600 ÷ 12 =

360 ÷ 12 =   720 ÷ 12 =   960 ÷ 12 =

1 Complete each mini multiplication square as quickly as you can.

x	7	3	12	6
9				
5				
8				
11				

x	4	9	10	5
6				
3				
7				
25				

2 Write the multiples of 7 between 50 and 100.

For the following questions, write each answer as a number with a remainder.

3 In a class of 30 children, how many groups of 4 children can be made? How many children will not be in a group of 4?

4 In a class of 30 children, how many groups of 9 children can be made? How many children will not be in a group of 9?

5 In a class of 30 children, how many groups of 8 children can be made? How many children will not be in a group of 8?

6 In a school of 103 children, how many groups of 4 children can be made? How many children will not be in a group of 4?

7 In a school of 103 children, how many groups of 6 children can be made? How many children will not be in a group of 6?

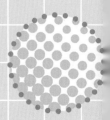

Short multiplication of three-digit numbers

This is where your times tables really help!

Look at this question:

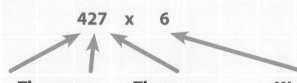

427 x 6

There are four hundreds.   **There are two tens.**   **There are seven units.**   **We are multiplying by six units.**

```
    4   2   7
x           6
_____
            2
_____
        4
```

```
    4   2   7
x           6
_____
        6   2
_____
    1   4
```

```
    4   2   7
x           6
_____
2   5   6   2
_____
    1   4
```

We multiply the 7 units by the 6 units first, which makes 42, so we write the 2 in the units column and carry the 4 to under the tens column.

Now we multiply the 2 tens by the 6 units to give 12. Add the 4 tens that were carried over so we now have 16 tens, which is enough for 1 hundred and 6 tens.

We carry the 1 hundred to under the hundreds column. Now we multiply the 4 hundreds by the 6 units to give 24 hundreds. Finally, we add the 1 hundred, so that we now have enough for 5 hundreds and 2 thousands.

Now try these.

1 379 x 8

3 738 x 6

2 523 x 4

4 567 x 9

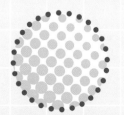

Use your times tables!

Can you multiply using three-digit numbers? Answer the questions below. The first one has been done for you.

1 798 x 3

```
    7   9   8
x           3
_____
2   3   9   4
    2   2
```

2 642 x 6

3 598 x 9

4 843 x 7

5 734 x 8

6 941 x 5

7 608 x 4

8 832 x 7

Brodie's Fast Five

15 x 9 =

15 x 8 =

15 x 6 =

15 x 4 =

15 x 7 =

Let's practise multiplying four-digit numbers by one-digit numbers.

Look at this question:

4683   x   4

| There are four thousands. | There are six hundreds. | There are eight tens. | There are three units. | We are multiplying by four units. |

Look at the stages involved in working out this multiplication.

①

	4	6	8	3
x				4
				2
			1	

②

	4	6	8	3
x				4
			3	2
		3	1	

③

	4	6	8	3
x				4
		7	3	2
	2	3	1	

④

	4	6	8	3
x				4
1	8	7	3	2
	2	3	1	

We multiply the 3 units by the 4 units first. Next, we work along the top line, multiplying the tens by the 4, then the hundreds by the 4, and finally the thousands by the 4.

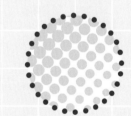

Now try these.

1 7342 x 7

3 2847 x 9

2 8493 x 6

4 5999 x 8

Are you confident using short multiplication?

Use short multiplication to answer the questions on this page.
The first one has been done for you.

1 7209 x 4

```
    7  2  0  9
x            4
_____
 2  8  8  3  6
          3
```

5 3753 x 8

2 8341 x 6

6 2098 x 5

3 9376 x 9

7 6394 x 4

4 7248 x 7

8 7878 x 7

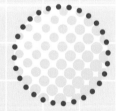

Brodie's Fast Five

10 x 18 =   20 x 18 =

30 x 18 =   40 x 18 =   50 x 18 =

Using short multiplication

Can you solve these problems?

A surveyor has worked out the quantities of materials needed to build one house. These are some of his results.

8765 bricks
9716 roof tiles
1702 metres of roofing batten

1 How many bricks would be needed to build three houses?

2 How many roof tiles would be needed to build three houses?

3 How many metres of roofing batten would be needed to build three houses?

4 How many bricks would be needed to build six houses?

5 How many roof tiles would be needed to build six houses?

6 How many metres of roofing batten would be needed to build six houses?

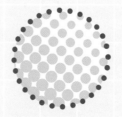

Use short multiplication to answer the questions on this page.

1 4679 x 3

4 9146 x 7

2 3584 x 7

5 5238 x 9

3 7748 x 8

6 7293 x 6

7 A surveyor has worked out the quantities of materials needed to build one house. These are some of his results.

8765 bricks
9716 roof tiles
1702 metres of roofing batten

How many bricks would be needed to build eight houses?

Short division reminder page

On this page we are dividing three-digit numbers.

Look at this question:

$$974 \div 2$$

There are nine hundreds.

There are seven tens.

There are four units.

We are dividing by two units.

Look at the stages involved in working out this division.

1

$$\begin{array}{c|ccc} & 4 & & \\ \hline 2 & 9 & {}^{1}7 & 4 \end{array}$$

2

$$\begin{array}{c|ccc} & 4 & 8 & \\ \hline 2 & 9 & {}^{1}7 & {}^{1}4 \end{array}$$

3

$$\begin{array}{c|ccc} & 4 & 8 & 7 \\ \hline 2 & 9 & {}^{1}7 & {}^{1}4 \end{array}$$

First, we divide the 9 by the 2, giving an answer of 4, which we write in the hundreds column. We have 1 left over, so we carry this over to the tens column and break it down into tens, giving a total of 17. Now we divide the 17 tens by the 2, giving an answer of 8 for the tens column and 1 ten to break into units. Finally we divide the 14 units by the 2, to gain a final answer of 487.

Now try these.

1 868 ÷ 4

3 807 ÷ 3

2 736 ÷ 2

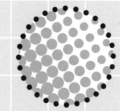

Brodie's Fast Five

480 ÷ 4 =   800 ÷ 4 =

600 ÷ 4 =   640 ÷ 4 =   760 ÷ 4 =

Short division

Can you remember how to divide three-digit numbers?

Use short division to answer the questions on this page.
The first one has been done for you.

1 816 ÷ 3

$$\begin{array}{c|cccc} & 2 & 7 & 2 \\ \hline 3 & 8 & {}^2 1 & 6 \end{array}$$

5 378 ÷ 2

2 968 ÷ 4

6 784 ÷ 4

3 865 ÷ 5

7 861 ÷ 7

4 912 ÷ 6

8 792 ÷ 4

Brodie's Fast Five

91 ÷ 7 =

75 ÷ 5 =

184 ÷ 2 =

156 ÷ 12 =

96 ÷ 2 =

Short division with remainders

Look carefully at the way we write out a short division.

Look at this question:

$$817 \div 5$$

Look at how the division is solved.

①

```
5 | 8  1  7
```

②

```
    1
5 | 8 ³1  7
```

③

```
    1  6
5 | 8 ³1 ¹7
```

④

```
    1  6  3  r2
5 | 8 ³1 ¹7
```

Use short division to answer the questions below.

1   723 ÷ 5

2   919 ÷ 5

3   397 ÷ 2

4   569 ÷ 7

5   789 ÷ 8

6   595 ÷ 6

Brodie's Fast Five

2 x 250 = ⬜   3 x 250 = ⬜

4 x 250 = ⬜   5 x 250 = ⬜   6 x 250 = ⬜

On this page we are dividing four-digit numbers.

Look at this question:

$$7348 \div 2$$

There are seven thousands.

There are three hundreds.

There are four tens.

There are eight units.

We are dividing by two units.

Look at how the question is solved.

Step ❶ Divide the thousands.

```
      1
   ┌─────────────
 4 │ 7  ³3  4  8
```

Step ❷ Divide the hundreds.

```
      1   8
   ┌─────────────
 4 │ 7  ³3  ¹4  ²8
```

Step ❸ Divide the tens.

```
      1   8   3
   ┌─────────────
 4 │ 7  ³3  ¹4  ²8
```

Step ❹ Divide the units.

```
      1   8   3   7
   ┌─────────────
 4 │ 7  ³3  ¹4  ²8
```

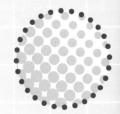

Now try these. Some of the questions may have remainders.

1 $3428 \div 4$

4 $9142 \div 8$

2 $5785 \div 5$

5 $7358 \div 9$

3 $4639 \div 7$

6 $8725 \div 6$

Short division problems

Use short division to answer the questions on this page.

A secondary school has 1348 pupils.

1 If the pupils are put into pairs, how many pairs would there be?

2 If the pupils are put into groups of three, how many groups would there be?

3 If the pupils are put into groups of four, how many groups would there be?

4 If the pupils are put into groups of five, how many groups would there be?

5 If the pupils are put into groups of six, how many groups would there be?

6 If the pupils are put into groups of seven, how many groups would there be?

7 If the pupils are put into groups of eight, how many groups would there be?

8 If the pupils are put into groups of nine, how many groups would there be?

Brodie's Fast Five

$6000 \div 4 =$ $7000 \div 4 =$

$8000 \div 4 =$ $9000 \div 4 =$ $10000 \div 4 =$

Use short division to answer the questions.

1 $7398 \div 4$

3 $3456 \div 2$

2 $5678 \div 6$

4 $8264 \div 7$

There are 852 sweets in a jar. They are going to be put into packets, with each packet containing the same number of sweets. Answer the questions below and give the remainders if there are any sweets left over.

5   How many sweets can be put in each of three packets?

7   How many sweets can be put in each of seven packets?

6   How many sweets can be put in each of six packets?

8   How many sweets can be put in each of nine packets?

Now answer these multiplication questions.

9 625×4

11 3416×10

10 1425×7

12 2479×9

We need to multiply by tens.

Look at this question:

43 x 20

As you know, when we multiply by 10, the digits in the number move one place to the left. We can show this in a formal written multiplication:

Step 1
Write the numbers above one another.

```
    4 3
x   2 0
_____
```

Step 2
Write a zero in the units column to automatically move the answer digits to the left.

```
    4 3
x   2 0
_____
      0
```

Step 3
Multiply the 3 units by the 2 tens and write the 6 in the tens column.

```
    4 3
x   2 0
_____
    6 0
```

Step 4
Multiply the 4 tens by the 2 tens and write the 8 in the hundreds column.

```
      4 3
x     2 0
_____
  8   6 0
```

Sometimes we need to 'carry' digits to the tens column or the hundreds column or the thousands column.

Look at this question:

67 x 40

Step 1
Write the numbers above one another.

```
    6 7
x   4 0
_____
```

Step 2
Write a zero in the units column to automatically move the answer digits to the left.

```
    6 7
x   4 0
_____
      0
```

Step 3
Multiply the 7 units by the 4 tens. Write the 8 in the tens column and carry the 2 to the hundreds.

```
    6 7
x   4 0
_____
    8 0
  2
```

Step 4
Multiply the 6 tens by the 4 tens. Add the 2, then write the 6 in the hundreds column and carry the 2 straight into the thousands column.

```
        6 7
x       4 0
_____
  2 6   8 0
    2
```

Multiplication by tens

Look carefully at the examples on page 21.

Use short multiplication to answer the questions on this page.
The first one has been done for you.

1   73 x 30

		7	3
x		3	0
2	1	9	0

5   146 x 80

2   59 x 60

6   299 x 40

3   82 x 90

7   137 x 50

4   67 x 70

8   679 x 70

Brodie's Fast Five

10 x 97 = ⬚   100 x 84 = ⬚

100 x 124 = ⬚   10 x 38 = ⬚   702 x 100 = ⬚

Long multiplication

We need to multiply by two-digit numbers.

Look at this question:

48   x   32

We need to multiply 48 by the 2 units first. We then multiply by the 3 tens, and add the two answers together. We can show this in one calculation:

```
            4   8
  x         3   2
  _____
            9   6     ← This row shows the multiplication of 48 x 2
            1
  1   4   4   0       ← This row shows the multiplication of 48 x 30
      2
  1   5   3   6       ← This row shows the two multiplications added
      1                  together.
```

Now try these.

1   73 x 26

3   93 x 47

2   86 x 34

4   64 x 59

More long multiplication

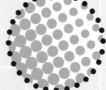

Look carefully at the examples on page 23.

Answer the long multiplication questions below.
The first one has been done for you.

1 58 x 24

```
          5   8
   x      2   4
   _____
      2   3   2
          3
   1   1   6   0
   _____
       1
   1   3   9   2
```

2 39 x 18

3 74 x 34

4 75 x 28

5 249 x 23

6 436 x 37

7 367 x 84

8 867 x 59

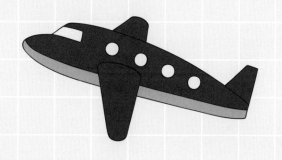

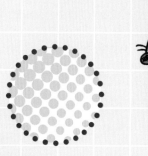

You may need an extra sheet of paper for your working.

1 Brodie Airways' fleet includes the following aeroplanes.
Complete the table to show the total number of
passengers that can be carried by each type of plane.

Type of plane	Number in fleet	Passenger capacity	Total number of passengers
Bluebird 777-300	12	299	
Kestrel 319-100	44	143	
Eagle 190	11	98	
Eagle 170	6	76	
Bluebird 747-400	42	345	
Bluebird 757-200	3	114	
Kestrel 321-200	18	205	

Brodie's Fast Five

20 x 20 =

30 x 30 =

40 x 40 =

50 x 50 =

60 x 60 =

Use short division to answer the questions.

1 Brodie Airways' fleet includes the following aeroplanes. Complete the table to show the total number of passengers that can be carried by each type of plane.

Type of plane	Number in fleet	Passenger capacity	Total number of passengers
Bluebird 777-200	46	280	
Kestrel 318-100	2	32	
Kestrel 320-200	62	174	
Kestrel 318-100	6	76	
Bluebird 767-300	14	252	
Bluebird 787-8	8	214	
Kestrel 380-800	11	469	

2 What is the maximum total number of passengers that can be carried on the Bluebird planes in this table?

3 What is the maximum total number of passengers that can be carried on the Kestrel planes in this table?

Factors

Can you find the factors of any number?

Look at the ways we can make 12 by multiplying.

1×12 6×2

12×1 — **12** — 3×4

2×6 4×3

We say that the factors of 12 are 1, 2, 3, 4, 6 and 12.

12 is in the 2 times table.   12 is in the 3 times table.   12 is in the 4 times table.

12 is in the 6 times table.   12 is in the 12 times table.

1   Write the multiplication facts for each number below.

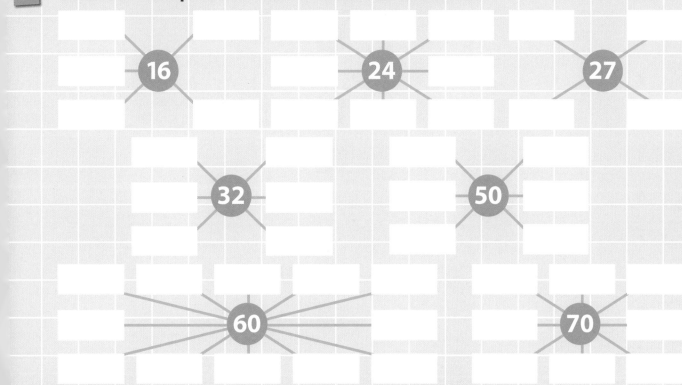

Use the multiplication facts to find all the factors of each number.

2   The factors of 16 are

3   The factors of 24 are

4   The factors of 27 are

5   The factors of 32 are

6   The factors of 50 are

7   The factors of 60 are

8   The factors of 70 are

Prime numbers

Some numbers have only two factors.

Look at the ways we can make 13 by multiplying.

$$1 \times 13 \longrightarrow 13 \longleftarrow 13 \times 1$$

The number 1 is a special number. Its only factor is itself.

Prime numbers have two factors. Number 13 is a prime number. It has only two factors: itself and 1. It is not in any multiplication table except its own table, the thirteens.

Write the factors for each number below.

1	2	11	12
2	3	12	29
3	4	13	36
4	5		
5	6		
6	7		
7	8	14	41
8	9	15	48
9	10		
10	11		

16 Numbers with only two factors, themselves and 1, are called prime numbers. Which of the numbers above are prime numbers?

Brodie's Fast Five

15 x 5 =   16 x 6 =

17 x 7 =   18 x 8 =   19 x 9 =

Here is a way to find prime numbers less than 100.

Look at the hundred square.

- **Cross out the number 1 because it is not a prime number.**
- **Leave number 2, as it is a prime number, but cross out every multiple of 2 all the way up to 100.**
- **Leave number 3, as it is a prime number, but cross out every multiple of 3.**
- **Leave number 5, as it is a prime number, but cross out every multiple of 5.**
- **Leave number 7, as it is a prime number, but cross out every multiple of 7.**

1	2	3	4	5	6	7	8	9	10
11	12	13	14	15	16	17	18	19	20
21	22	23	24	25	26	27	28	29	30
31	32	33	34	35	36	37	38	39	40
41	42	43	44	45	46	47	48	49	50
51	52	53	54	55	56	57	58	59	60
61	62	63	64	65	66	67	68	69	70
71	72	73	74	75	76	77	78	79	80
81	82	83	84	85	86	87	88	89	90
91	92	93	94	95	96	97	98	99	100

1 **Which numbers are not crossed out?**

2 **What is the only even prime number?**

Brodie's Fast Five

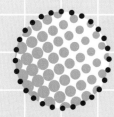

36 ÷ 12 =

360 ÷ 12 =

3600 ÷ 12 =

48 ÷ 12 =

4800 ÷ 12 =

Square numbers

 Multiplying a number by itself makes a square number.

Look at the dot patterns.

One set of one.	Two sets of two.	Three sets of three.	Four sets of four.
1 x 1 = 1	2 x 2 = 4	3 x 3 = 9	4 x 4 = 16

The numbers 1, 4, 9 and 16 are all square numbers.
The next square number is 25.
Look: 5 x 5 = 25
We can write this like this: $5^2 = 25$

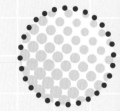

Now try these.

1 $6^2 =$ 5 $10^2 =$ 9 $70^2 =$

2 $7^2 =$ 6 $11^2 =$ 10 $80^2 =$

3 $8^2 =$ 7 $12^2 =$ 11 $90^2 =$

4 $9^2 =$ 8 $20^2 =$ 12 $100^2 =$

You will need to use long multiplication for the next questions.

13 13^2 16 16^2

14 14^2 17 17^2

15 15^2 18 18^2

Cube numbers

Look at the cubes.

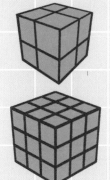

This cube is made of 8 small cubes. It is two little cubes wide. It is two little cubes deep. It is two little cubes high. $2 \times 2 \times 2 = 8$

This cube is made of 27 small cubes. It is three little cubes wide. It is three little cubes deep. It is three little cubes high. $3 \times 3 \times 3 = 27$

The numbers 8 and 27 are called cube numbers. The next cube number is 64.

Now try these. You may need to use short multiplication or long multiplication or you may need to complete two long multiplications to find some of the answers.

1 5^3

2 6^3

3 7^3

4 8^3

5 9^3

6 10^3

7 16^3

8 64^3

How quickly can you complete all of these questions?

1 What are the factors of 96?

2 Draw a ring around the prime number: 15   19   21   25   27

3 What are the factors of 200?

4 Draw a ring around the prime number: 31   32   33   34   35

5 What are the factors of 1000?

6 Draw a ring around the prime number: 91   92   93   95   97

7 16^2

9 6^3

8 24^2

10 32^3

Long division

Sometimes we need to use long division.

Look at this question:

$$756 \div 12$$

There are seven hundreds.

There are five tens.

There are six units.

We are dividing by twelve.

Step ❶

We try to divide the 7 hundreds by the 12 first, but 7 is less than 12 so we combine the 7 hundreds with the 5 tens. We can then divide 75 by 12, writing the 6 of the answer in the tens column.

```
        6
1  2 | 7  5  6
```

Step ❷

As we just worked out, 12 goes into 75 six times. This gets us to 72, with a remainder of 3. In long division, we show our working by subtracting the 72 from the 75, and writing the 3 underneath.

```
        6
1  2 | 7  5  6
   -   7  2
          3
```

Step ❸

Now we bring down the 6 units and write it below the line, next to the 3, to give 36. 36 divided by 12 is exactly 3. The final answer is 63.

```
        6  3
1  2 | 7  5  6
   -   7  2
          3  6
```

With the questions below it can help to write out the multiples of the divisor. (Divisors are the numbers we are dividing by.) For the first question, for example, you could write out the multiples of 16 so that you can count how many sixteens are needed to answer each part of the question.

Here are the multiples of 16 up to 9 x 16:

16 32 48 64 80 96 112 128 144

1 $768 \div 16$

2 $966 \div 23$

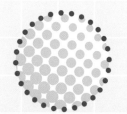

More long division

This division is even longer than the last!

Look at this question:

$$2508 \div 19$$

Step ❶
We try to divide the 2 thousands by the 19 first, but 2 is less than 19 so we combine the 2 thousands with the 5 hundreds and divide 25 by 19. We write the 1 of the answer in the hundreds column.

Step ❷
As we just worked out, 19 goes into 25 once, with a remainder of 6. We show our working by subtracting the 19 from the 25, and writing the 6 underneath. Now we bring down the 0 and write it next to the 6 to give 60. 19 goes into 60 three times, to make 57, with a remainder of 3.

Step ❸
We show our working by subtracting the 57 from the 60, then by drawing another answer line and writing the 3 underneath. Next, we bring the 8 down next to the 3, to give 38. 38 divided by 19 is 2, so the final answer is 132.

```
            1
1  9 | 2   5   0   8
```

```
                1   3
1  9 | 2   5   0   8
     -   1   9
         -   6   0
```

```
                1   3   2
1  9 | 2   5   0   8
     -   1   9
         -   6   0
             5   7
                 3   8
```

Now try these. Don't forget, you may like to write out the multiples of the divisors. (Divisors are the numbers we are dividing by.)

1 $8892 \div 26$

2 $9102 \div 37$

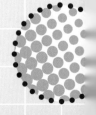

This long division has a remainder.

Look at this question:

$$14205 \div 36$$

Here are the multiples of 36 up to 9 x 36, which may help you:

36 72 108 144 180 216 252 288 324

Look carefully at each step.

1

```
              3
    3 6 | 1 4 2 0 5
```

2

```
              3
    3 6 | 1 4 2 0 5
        - 1 0 8
            3 4
```

3

```
              3 9
    3 6 | 1 4 2 0 5
        - 1 0 8
            3 4 0
          - 3 2 4
```

4

```
              3 9 4
    3 6 | 1 4 2 0 5
        - 1 0 8
            3 4 0
          - 3 2 4
              1 6 5
              1 4 4
                2 1 r
```

The letter r is written next to the 21 to show that it is the remainder. So, the final answer is 394 r21.

Now try these. Don't forget, you may like to write out the multiples of the divisors.

1 7750 ÷ 29

2 29154 ÷ 43

Long division practice

Use long division to answer the questions on this page.

The first question has been done for you.

1   **587 ÷ 23**

```
            2  5
   2  3 | 5  8  7
       -  4  6
          1  2  7
          1  1  5
             1  2  r
```

2   **748 ÷ 24**

3   **688 ÷ 43**

4   **2695 ÷ 32**

5   **9847 ÷ 64**

6   **23142 ÷ 58**

Can you solve the problems?

You may need to use addition or subtraction as well as multiplication.

Cathy's Coach Company has some 38-seat coaches and some 56-seat coaches. It costs £145 to hire a 38-seat coach for a day and £195 to hire a 56-seat coach.

1 A secondary school has 1892 pupils. All the pupils are travelling to a sports ground. How many 38-seat coaches would be needed? Remember, no pupils can be left out!

4 What would be the total cost of hiring the 56-seat coaches?

2 If the same school could hire only the 56-seat coaches, how many would be needed?

5 Which would be the cheaper option?

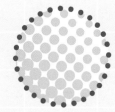

3 What would be the total cost of hiring the 38-seat coaches?

6 How much cheaper would it be?

How quickly can you complete all of these questions?

1   882 ÷ 18

3   9724 ÷ 37

2   24564 ÷ 46

4   17468 ÷ 34

5   A school has 1456 pupils. It has 7 minibuses, each of which can seat 16 pupils. How many trips would be needed to transport all of the pupils?

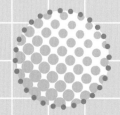

Multiplying or dividing by 10

Multiplying by 10 moves all digits one place to the left.

Look at these multiplications by 10.

$4 \times 10 = 40$ $37 \times 10 = 370$ $416 \times 10 = 4160$ $2798 \times 10 = 27980$

Now try these.

1 $46 \times 10 =$

2 $38 \times 10 =$

3 $458 \times 10 =$

4 $2740 \times 10 =$

Look at these multiplications by 10.

$0.7 \times 10 = 7$ $5.8 \times 10 = 58$ $7.39 \times 10 = 73.9$ $6.425 \times 10 = 64.25$

Now try these.

5 $0.9 \times 10 =$

6 $7.2 \times 10 =$

7 $9.65 \times 10 =$

8 $0.369 \times 10 =$

Look at these divisions by 10.

$8 \div 10 = 0.8$ $37 \div 10 = 3.7$ $265 \div 10 = 26.5$ $4798 \div 10 = 479.8$

Now try these.

9 $5 \div 10 =$

10 $79 \div 10 =$

11 $547 \div 10 =$

12 $3649 \div 10 =$

Look at these divisions by 10.

$0.7 \div 10 = 0.07$ $5.8 \div 10 = 0.58$ $12.56 \div 10 = 1.256$ $6.425 \div 10 = 0.6425$

Now try these.

13 $0.2 \div 10 =$

14 $8.4 \div 10 =$

15 $2.47 \div 10 =$

16 $28.28 \div 10 =$

Brodie's Fast Five

$78 \times 10 =$ $78 \div 10 =$

$180 \times 10 =$ $97 \div 10 =$ $0.97 \times 10 =$

39

Multiplying by 100 moves all digits two places to the left.

Look at these multiplications by 100.

3 x 100 = 300   23 x 100 = 2300   567 x 100 = 56700   3684 x 100 = 368400

Now try these.

1 17 x 100 =

2 86 x 100 =

3 237 x 100 =

4 2006 x 100 =

Look at these multiplications by 100.

0.6 x 100 = 60   3.8 x 100 = 380   6.46 x 100 = 646   0.318 x 100 = 31.8

Now try these.

5 0.8 x 100 =

6 6.2 x 100 =

7 12.65 x 100 =

8 7.246 x 100 =

Look at these divisions by 100.

7 ÷ 100 = 0.07   56 ÷ 100 = 0.56   265 ÷ 100 = 2.65   8234 ÷ 100 = 82.34

Now try these.

9 6 ÷ 100 =

10 24 ÷ 100 =

11 789 ÷ 100 =

12 5246 ÷ 100 =

Look at these divisions by 100.

0.7 ÷ 100 = 0.007   4.8 ÷ 100 = 0.048   34.2 ÷ 100 = 0.342   126.4 ÷ 100 = 1.264

Now try these.

13 0.2 ÷ 100 =

14 7.9 ÷ 100 =

15 34.6 ÷ 100 =

16 548.6 ÷ 100 =

Brodie's Fast Five

56 x 100 =   56 ÷ 100 =

270 x 100 =   48 ÷ 100 =   0.001 x 100 =

Multiplying or dividing by 1000

Multiplying by 1000 moves all digits three places to the left.

Look at these multiplications by 1000.

3 x 1000 = 3000   52 x 1000 = 52000   319 x 1000 = 319000   2500 x 1000 = 2500000

Now try these.

1   9 x 1000 =

2   42 x 1000 =

3   675 x 1000 =

4   1095 x 1000 =

Look at these multiplications by 1000.

0.4 x 1000 = 400   4.8 x 1000 = 4800   3.72 x 1000 = 3720   6.297 x 1000 = 6297

Now try these.

5   0.1 x 1000 =

6   3.9 x 1000 =

7   48.32 x 1000 =

8   5.624 x 1000 =

Look at these divisions by 1000.

3 ÷ 1000 = 0.003   29 ÷ 1000 = 0.029   814 ÷ 1000 = 0.814   6523 ÷ 1000 = 6.523

Now try these.

9   7 ÷ 1000 =

10   63 ÷ 1000 =

11   654 ÷ 1000 =

12   4850 ÷ 1000 =

13   195 ÷ 1000 =

14   9236 ÷ 1000 =

15   18 ÷ 1000=

16   42 ÷ 1000 =

Brodie's Fast Five

18000 ÷ 1000 =

1800 ÷ 1000 =

180 ÷ 1000 =

18 ÷ 1000 =

36 ÷ 1000 =

We need to be able to multiply decimals by whole numbers.

Look at this question:

$$0.4 \quad x \quad 6 \quad = \quad 2.4$$

Because this number has one decimal place...

... and we are multiplying by a whole number...

... the answer has one decimal place.

Now try these.

1	0.7 x 8 =		**6**	0.8 x 8 =	
2	0.4 x 9 =		**7**	0.4 x 5 =	
3	0.5 x 7 =		**8**	0.1 x 6 =	
4	0.2 x 6 =		**9**	0.6 x 6 =	
5	0.3 x 9 =		**10**	0.7 x 3 =	

Look at this multiplication.

$$0.04 \quad x \quad 6 \quad = \quad 0.24$$

Because this number has two decimal places...

... and we are multiplying by a whole number...

... the answer has two decimal places.

Now try these.

11	0.04 x 8 =		**16**	0.04 x 8 =	
12	0.05 x 9 =		**17**	0.07 x 5 =	
13	0.06 x 7 =		**18**	0.09 x 6 =	
14	0.09 x 6 =		**19**	0.08 x 6 =	
15	0.02 x 9 =		**20**	0.03 x 3 =	

More multiplication of decimals

Don't forget the decimal point in each answer.

Look at this question:

$$0.3 \times 48 =$$

With this question, it is easier to complete the short multiplication 48 x 3 to reach the answer 144 then to put the decimal point back in. Because there is one decimal place in the question, there has to be one decimal place in the answer so the final answer is 14.4

Now try these.

1 0.6 x 27 =

6 0.4 x 123 =

2 0.9 x 63 =

7 732 x 0.5 =

3 36 x 0.7 =

8 0.2 x 947 =

4 72 x 0.8 =

9 2473 x 0.6 =

5 89 x 0.3 =

10 0.4 x 8392 =

Did you notice that the answer to question 7 is half of 732? This is because the decimal 0.5 is worth the same as ½.

How quickly can you complete all of these questions?

1 0.6 x 10 =

2 9.34 x 10 =

3 0.298 x 10 =

4 642 ÷ 10 =

5 4745 ÷ 10 =

6 0.6 ÷ 10 =

7 0.3 x 100 =

8 0.3 ÷ 100 =

9 5.9 ÷ 100 =

10 29.34 x 1000 =

11 8348 ÷ 1000 =

12 7 x 0.04 =

13 0.9 x 47

14 64 x 0.6

15 0.3 x 78

ANSWERS

Page 3 • Practising the times tables: 2, 3, 4 and 5

1.
2	3	4	5
4	6	8	10
6	9	12	15
8	12	16	20
10	15	20	25
12	18	24	30
14	21	28	35
16	24	32	40
18	27	36	45
20	30	40	50
22	33	44	55
24	36	48	60

2. 4 8 12 16 20 24 28 32 36 40
44 48 52 56 60 64 68 72 76
80 84 88 92 96 100
3. 5 10 15 20 25 30 35 40 45
50 55 60 65 70 75 80 85 90
95 100

Page 4 • Practising the times tables: 6, 7, 8 and 9

1.
6	7	8	9
12	14	16	18
18	21	24	27
24	28	32	36
30	35	40	45
36	42	48	54
42	49	56	63
48	56	64	72
54	63	72	81
60	70	80	90
66	77	88	99
72	84	96	108

2. 7 14 21 28 35 42 49 56 63
70 77 84 91 98
3. 8 16 24 32 40 48 56 64 72
80 88 96
4. 9 18 27 36 45 54 63 72 81
90 99

Page 5 • Practising the times tables: 10, 11, 12 and 25

1.
10	11	12	25
20	22	24	50
30	33	36	75
40	44	48	100
50	55	60	125
60	66	72	150
70	77	84	175
80	88	96	200
90	99	108	225
100	110	120	250
110	121	132	275
120	132	144	300

2. 11 22 33 44 55 66 77 88 99
110 121 132 143 154 165
176 187 198
3. 12 24 36 48 60 72 84 96
108 120 132 144 156 168
180 192
4. 25 50 75 100 125 150 175
200 225 250 275 300 325
350 375 400 425 450 475
500

Page 6 • Mixed multiplication square

x	7	3	6	4	9	12	8	11	2	5	10	25
8	56	24	48	32	72	96	64	88	16	40	80	200
11	77	33	66	44	99	132	88	121	22	55	110	275
3	21	9	18	12	27	36	24	33	6	15	30	75
10	70	30	60	40	90	120	80	110	20	50	100	250
5	35	15	30	20	45	60	40	55	10	25	50	125
9	63	27	54	36	81	108	72	99	18	45	90	225
2	14	6	12	8	18	24	16	22	4	10	20	50
7	49	21	42	28	63	84	56	77	14	35	70	175
12	84	36	72	48	108	144	96	132	24	60	120	300
6	42	18	36	24	54	72	48	66	12	30	60	150
25	175	75	150	100	225	300	200	275	50	125	250	625
4	28	12	24	16	36	48	32	44	8	20	40	100

Brodie's Fast Five
1. 50
2. 16
3. 5
4. 6
5. 15

Page 7 • Divisions with remainders

1. 12 r3
2. 8 r2
3. 12 r3
4. 13 r5
5. 7 r4
6. 13 r3
7. 12 r4
8. 9 r8
9. 4 r1
10. 8 r5
11. 9 r2
12. 50 r1
13. 12 r5
14. 25 r1
15. 16 r5
16. 20 r1
17. 3 r11
18. 2 r21

Brodie's Fast Five
1. 20
2. 50
3. 30
4. 60
5. 80

Page 8 • Progress Test 1

1.

x	7	3	12	6
9	63	27	108	54
5	35	15	60	30
8	56	24	96	48
11	77	33	132	66

x	4	9	10	5
6	24	54	60	30
3	12	27	30	15
7	28	63	70	35
25	100	225	250	125

2. 56 63 70 77 84 91 98
3. 7 groups of 4, with 2 children left
4. 3 groups of 9, with 3 children left
5. 3 groups of 8, with 6 children left
6. 25 groups of 4, with 3 children left
7. 17 groups of 6, with 1 child left

Page 9 • Short multiplication of three-digit numbers

1. 3032
2. 2092
3. 4428
4. 5103

Page 10 • More short multiplication of three-digit numbers

1. 2394
2. 3852
3. 5382
4. 5901
5. 5872
6. 4705
7. 2432
8. 5824

Brodie's Fast Five
1. 135
2. 120
3. 90
4. 60
5. 105

Page 11 • Short multiplication of four-digit numbers

1. 51394
2. 50958
3. 25623
4. 47992

Page 12 • More short multiplication of four-digit numbers

1. 28836
2. 50046
3. 84384
4. 50736
5. 30024
6. 10490
7. 25576
8. 55146

Brodie's Fast Five

1. 180
2. 360
3. 540
4. 720
5. 900

Page 13 • Using short multiplication

1. 26295
2. 29148
3. 5106
4. 52590
5. 58296
6. 10212

Page 14 • Progress Test 2

1. 14037
2. 25088
3. 61984
4. 64022
5. 47142
6. 43758
7. 70120

Page 15 • Short division reminder page

1. 217
2. 368
3. 269

Brodie's Fast Five

1. 120
2. 200
3. 150
4. 160
5. 190

Page 16 • Short division

1. 272
2. 242
3. 173
4. 152
5. 189
6. 196
7. 123
8. 198

Brodie's Fast Five

1. 13
2. 15
3. 92
4. 13
5. 48

Page 17 • Short division with remainders

1. 144 r3
2. 183 r4
3. 198 r1
4. 81 r2
5. 98 r5
6. 99 r1

Brodie's Fast Five

1. 500
2. 750
3. 1000
4. 1250
5. 1500

Page 18 • Short division of four-digit numbers

1. 857
2. 1157
3. 662 r5
4. 1142 r6
5. 817 r5
6. 1454 r1

Page 19 • Short division problems

1. 674
2. 449 with 1 pupil left out of a group
3. 337
4. 269 with 3 pupils left out of a group
5. 224 with 4 pupils left out of a group
6. 192 with 4 pupils left out of a group
7. 168 with 4 pupils left out of a group
8. 149 with 7 pupils left out of a group

Brodie's Fast Five

1. 1500
2. 1750
3. 2000
4. 2250
5. 2500

Page 20 • Progress Test 3

1. 1849 r2
2. 946 r2
3. 1728
4. 1180 r4

5. 284
6. 142
7. 121 r5
8. 94 r6

9. 2500
10. 9975
11. 34160
12. 22311

Page 22 • Multiplication by tens

1. 2190
2. 3540
3. 7380
4. 4690
5. 11680
6. 11960
7. 6850
8. 47530

Brodie's Fast Five

1. 970
2. 8400
3. 12400
4. 380
5. 70200

Page 23 • Long multiplication

1. 1898
2. 2924
3. 4371
4. 3776

Page 24 • More long multiplication

1. 1392
2. 702
3. 2516
4. 2100
5. 5727
6. 16132
7. 30828
8. 51153

Page 25 • Using long multiplication

1.
Bluebird 777-300 3588
Kestrel 319-100 46292
Eagle 190 1078
Eagle 170 456
Bluebird 747-400 14490
Bluebird 757-200 342
Kestrel 321-200 3690

Brodie's Fast Five

1. 400
2. 900
3. 1600
4. 2500
5. 3600

Page 26 • Progress Test 4

1.
Bluebird 777-200 12880
Kestrel 318-100 64
Kestrel 320-200 10788
Kestrel 318-100 456
Bluebird 767-300 3528
Bluebird 787-8 1712
Kestrel 380-800 5159

2. 18120
3. 16467

Page 27 • Factors

1. 1 x 16, 16 x 1, 2 x 8, 8 x 2, 4 x 4
   1 x 24, 24 x 1, 2 x 12, 12 x 2,
   3 x 8, 8 x 3, 4 x 6, 6 x 4,
   1 x 27, 27 x 1, 3 x 9, 9 x 3
   1 x 32, 32 x 1, 2 x 16, 16 x 2,
   4 x 8, 8 x 4
   1 x 50, 50 x 1, 2 x 25, 25 x 2,
   5 x 10, 10 x 5
   1 x 60, 60 x 1, 2 x 30, 30 x 2,
   3 x 20, 20 x 3, 4 x 15, 15 x 4,
   5 x 12, 12 x 5, 6 x 10, 10 x 6
   1 x 70, 70 x 1, 2 x 35, 35 x 2,
   5 x 14, 14 x 5, 7 x 10, 10 x 7
2. 1 2 4 8 16
3. 1 2 3 4 6 8 12 24
4. 1 3 9 27
5. 1 2 4 8 16 32
6. 1 2 5 10 25 50
7. 1 2 3 4 5 6 10 12 15 20 30 60
8. 1 2 5 7 10 14 35 70

Page 28 • Prime numbers

1. 1 2
2. 1 3
3. 1 2 4
4. 1 5
5. 1 2 3 6
6. 1 7
7. 1 2 4 8
8. 1 3 9
9. 1 2 5 10
10. 1 11
11. 1 2 3 4 6 12
12. 1 29
13. 1 2 3 4 6 9 12 18 36
14. 1 41
15. 1 2 3 4 6 8 12 16 24 48
16. 2 3 5 7 11 29 41

Brodie's Fast Five

1. 75
2. 96
3. 119
4. 144
5. 171

Page 29 • Finding all the prime numbers up to 100

1. 2 3 5 7 11 13 17 19 23 29 31 37 41 43 47 53 59 61 67 71 73 79 83 89 97
2. 2

Brodie's Fast Five

1. 3
2. 30
3. 300
4. 4
5. 400

Page 30 • Square numbers

1. 36
2. 49
3. 64
4. 81
5. 100
6. 121
7. 144
8. 400
9. 4900
10. 6400
11. 8100
12. 10000
13. 169
14. 196
15. 225
16. 256
17. 289
18. 324

Page 31 • Cube numbers

1. 125
2. 216
3. 343
4. 512
5. 729
6. 1000
7. 4096
8. 262144

Page 32 • Progress Test 5

1. 1 2 3 4 6 8 12 16 24 32 48 96
2. 15 (19) 21 25 27 (circle 19)
3. 1 2 4 5 8 10 20 25 40 50 100 200
4. (31) 32 33 34 35
5. 1 2 4 5 8 10 20 25 40 50 100 125 200 250 500 1000
6. 91 92 93 95 (97)
7. 256
8. 576
9. 216
10. 32768

Page 33 • Long division

1. 48
2. 42

Page 34 • More long division

1. 342
2. 246

Page 35 • Long divisions with remainders

1. 267 r7
2. 678

Page 36 • Long division practice

1. 25 r12
2. 31 r4
3. 16
4. 84 r7
5. 153 r55
6. 399

Page 37 • Long division and multiplication problems

1. 50 coaches
2. 34 coaches
3. £7250
4. £6630
5. The 56-seat coaches
6. £620

Page 38 • Progress Test 6

1. 49
2. 534
3. 262 r30
4. 513 r26
5. 13

Page 39 • Multiplying or dividing by 10

1. 460
2. 380
3. 4580
4. 27400
5. 9
6. 72
7. 96.5
8. 3.69
9. 0.5
10. 7.9
11. 54.7
12. 364.9
13. 0.02
14. 0.84
15. 0.247
16. 2.828

Brodie's Fast Five

1. 780
2. 7.8
3. 1800
4. 9.7
5. 9.7

Page 40 • Multiplying or dividing by 100

1. 1700
2. 8600
3. 23700
4. 200600
5. 80
6. 620
7. 1265
8. 724.6
9. 0.06
10. 0.24
11. 7.89
12. 52.46
13. 0.002
14. 0.079
15. 0.346
16. 5.486

Brodie's Fast Five

1. 5600
2. 0.56
3. 27000
4. 0.48
5. 0.1

Page 41 • by 1000

1. 9000
2. 42000
3. 675000
4. 1095000
5. 100
6. 3900
7. 48320
8. 5624
9. 0.007
10. 0.063
11. 0.654
12. 4.85
13. 0.195
14. 9.236
15. 0.018
16. 0.042

Brodie's Fast Five

1. 18
2. 1.8
3. 0.18
4. 0.018
5. 0.036

Page 42 • Multiplication of decimals

1. 5.6
2. 3.6
3. 3.5
4. 1.2
5. 2.7
6. 6.4
7. 2
8. 0.6
9. 3.6
10. 2.1
11. 0.32
12. 0.45
13. 0.42
14. 0.54
15. 0.18
16. 0.32
17. 0.35
18. 0.54
19. 0.48
20. 0.09

Brodie's Fast Five

1. 360
2. 90
3. 90
4. 90
5. 540

Page 43 • More multiplication of decimals

1. 16.2
2. 56.7
3. 25.2
4. 57.6
5. 26.7
6. 49.2
7. 366
8. 189.4
9. 1483.8
10. 3356.8

Page 44 • Progress Test 7

1. 6
2. 93.4
3. 2.98
4. 64.2
5. 474.5
6. 0.06
7. 30
8. 0.003
9. 0.059
10. 29340
11. 8.348
12. 0.28
13. 42.3
14. 38.4
15. 23.4